COMPLETE TRAVEL GUIDE TO

NORTH RHINE-WESTPHALIA:

The most populous of the 16 component states of Germany, located in the west of the country.

Melly kelvin.

TABLE OF CONTENTS.

INTRODUCTION.

Greetings from North Rhine-Westphalia, a fascinating part of western Germany that mixes history, culture, and stunning natural scenery. This travel guide will lead you on a memorable tour across this varied and enthralling state, stopping at bustling cities and stunning scenery.

The most populous state in Germany and the location of several alluring locations is North Rhine-Westphalia, or NRW for short. Its lengthy history spans many centuries, with influences from the early industrialists, medieval knights, and ancient Romans helping to shape its personality. Today, NRW is known for its peaceful fusion of history and modernity, providing a wide range of experiences for all kinds of tourists.

Some of Germany's most vibrant cities are on display in NRW for urban explorers. Begin your journey in Cologne, which is famed for its magnificent cathedral and is listed as a UNESCO World Heritage site. Explore the busy streets that are dotted with lively cafés, hip shops, and old-fashioned attractions. Enjoy a delicious Kölsch beer, a specialty created only in Cologne, while you're there.

Continue traveling until you reach Düsseldorf, the regional center of commerce and fashion. A cosmopolitan metropolis with a thriving arts scene, upscale retail areas, and a top-notch culinary culture can be found here. Explore the lively Altstadt (Old Town), stroll along the lovely Rhine promenade, and savor the Museum Kunstpalast's world-class art collections.

North Rhine-Westphalia has a wide range of breathtaking natural beauties outside of the cities. The gorgeous scenery of the Eifel and Rhine Valley regions offers a tranquil respite from the bustle of the city. Take a picturesque hike through lush woods, look for hidden castles situated on hilltops, or take a boat ride down the flowing river to take in the stunning views.

NRW is a veritable gold mine of important historical sites for history buffs. Discover the historic city of Xanten, where the Archaeological Park brings the Roman era to life. Enter the medieval era in Aachen, where Charlemagne once lived, and be amazed by the intricate details of the Aachen Cathedral, a UNESCO World Heritage site. Explore the Ruhr region's industrial past by going to the Zollverein Coal Mine, a recognizable representation of the region's development.

The dynamic arts scene in NRW will enthrall culture buffs. Renowned institutions like the Kunstakademie Düsseldorf, a notable art school that has produced significant artists, and the Museum Ludwig in Cologne, which has a significant collection of modern and contemporary art, are both located in the area. Visit the Deutsche Oper am Rhein for enthralling performances or take part in one of the many annual traditional festivals to celebrate with friends and family.

North Rhine-Westphalia delivers a rich and varied travel experience, whether you're a history buff, a nature lover, or a cultural aficionado. Get ready to see the region's attractive cities, awe at its natural splendor, and learn about its fascinating history. This travel guide will provide you all the details you want to enjoy your trip through this captivating region of Germany. Pack your luggage and get ready for a journey that will give you lifelong memories of North Rhine-Westphalia.

CHAPTER 1.

I'll presume you're beginning your travel from a large city in another nation in order to give you a precise estimate for the cost of transportation to North Rhine-Westphalia. Please be aware that real prices may vary depending on the distance traveled, the form of transportation used, the time of year it is traveled, and whether or not discounts or special offers are available.

In addition, pricing for tickets and currency rates are subject to change. However, I will give you a broad estimate based on typical travel possibilities. Consider the following examples:

Explanation 1: A journey from London, England, to North Rhine-Westphalia, Germany journey: Ticket prices for a one-way journey in economy class between London and Düsseldorf International Airport may vary from $100 to $300, depending on the airline, the time of year you book, and space available.

rail: From the Düsseldorf Airport, you may travel by rail to several North Rhine-Westphalian cities, such Cologne or Dortmund. Depending on the route and train type, the rail cost might be anywhere from $15 and $50.

Local transit: Once you've reached your selected city, you may need to take local transit to go to your destination in North Rhine-Westphalia. In most places, a single ride on public transportation costs between $2 and $5.

Explanation 2: A journey from New York City, USA, to North Rhine-Westphalia, Germany

trip: Ticket prices for a one-way economy class trip from New York to Düsseldorf International Airport may vary from $400 to $800, depending on the airline, the time of year you book, and the number of seats available.
rail: From the Düsseldorf Airport, you may travel by rail to several North Rhine-Westphalian cities, such Cologne or Dortmund.

Depending on the route and train type, the rail cost might be anywhere from $15 and $50.
Local Transportation: Like the previous scenario, local transportation within the cities of North Rhine-Westphalia would cost between $2 and $5 each journey.

A third example is a trip from Sydney, Australia, to North Rhine-Westphalia, Germany:

trip: Ticket prices for a one-way economy class trip in the range of $1,000 to $2,000 are available from Sydney to Düsseldorf International Airport, depending on the airline, the time of year you book, and availability.

rail: From the Düsseldorf Airport, you may travel by rail to several North Rhine-Westphalian cities, such Cologne or Dortmund. Depending on the route and train type, the rail cost might be anywhere from $15 and $50.

Local transportation costs between $2 and $5 each journey inside the cities of North Rhine-Westphalia, as was previously noted.

Please be aware that these estimates are based on current pricing and might fluctuate dependent on things like currency rates, the time of booking, and seasonal variations. Before making any trip plans, it is usually important to inquire about the most precise and recent pricing with airlines, railway operators, and local transit providers.

__five budget-friendly hotels in North Rhine-Westphalia.__

Address for Ibis Budget Dortmund West is Provinzialstraße 396, Dortmund, Germany.

Walter-Gropius-Straße 11, 51147 Cologne, Germany is the address of the Hotel B&B Köln-Porz Airport.

Königswall 2, 44137 Dortmund, Germany is where B&B Hotel Dortmund-City is located.

Address for Hotel Premiere Classe Köln-West in Cologne, Germany is Brühler Str. 79, 50968

Address for the Hotel ibis Budget Dortmund Airport is Schleefstraße 2c, Dortmund, Germany, 44287.

Certainly! Here are five romantic hotels in North Rhine-Westphalia, Germany:

Brenners Park-Hotel & Spa is a luxurious hotel with a world-class spa that is situated in Baden-Baden, close to the North Rhine-Westphalia border. It provides a romantic environment with its lovely park location and magnificent rooms.

Hotel am Wasserturm: Located in Cologne, this distinctive hotel is constructed in a former water tower and offers attractive, roomy rooms with a combination of contemporary style and adornments for romance. Panoramic views of the city are available from the rooftop patio.

The castle hotel Schlosshotel Hugenpoet in Essen offers a very lovely setting. The hotel, which is located in a scenic area, has opulent accommodations, a fine-dining restaurant, and lovely gardens where couples may go for intimate strolls.

Althoff Grandhotel Schloss Bensberg - Located in Bergisch Gladbach, close to Cologne, this opulent castle hotel provides a fanciful atmosphere with mesmerizing views of the surroundings. The hotel has a Michelin-starred restaurant, a spa, and exquisite accommodations.

In Isselburg, close to the Dutch border, you'll find the romantic Parkhotel Wasserburg Anholt. It is located within a beautiful park that is encircled by a medieval castle with a moat. The hotel gives guests access to the castle grounds as well as pleasant accommodations and a charming restaurant.

North Rhine-Westphalia is a state in Germany known for its vibrant nightlife scene. Here are some of the best locations for nightlife in North Rhine-Westphalia:

A wide variety of nightlife alternatives are available in Düsseldorf, the state's main city. The various taverns, pubs, and clubs of the Altstadt (Old Town) are especially well-known. Another well-liked neighborhood is Medienhafen, which has hip pubs and eateries.

Cologne is a significant city in North Rhine-Westphalia and is known for its vibrant nightlife. Hip pubs and clubs may be found in the Belgian Quarter (Belgisches Viertel). Traditional breweries and beer halls may be found in the Old Town (Altstadt).

Dortmund: Particularly in the Westenhellweg and Brückstraße neighborhoods, Dortmund is noted for its vibrant nightlife. The city is home to several nightclubs, pubs, and music venues that may accommodate all preferences.

Essen: The Rüttenscheider Straße, which is surrounded by pubs, restaurants, and clubs, is the focus of this city's booming nightlife. Theaters, music venues, and art exhibits are also available in the city's cultural landscape.

Bonn: Although it is often mentioned in relation to its political importance, Bonn also boasts a vibrant nightlife. The Altstadt and Poppelsdorf neighborhoods, in particular, include a variety of taverns, clubs, and live music venues.

Aachen boasts a thriving nightlife in addition to being noted for its historical monuments. A mix of residents and students are drawn to the Pontstraße because of its abundance of taverns, clubs, and eateries.

Münster: Due to the city's substantial student population, Münster boasts a thriving nightlife. pubs and clubs may be found in the Kuhviertel and Hansaviertel neighborhoods, and there are waterfront cafés and pubs in the harbor neighborhood (Hafen).

Bochum: There is a thriving nightlife in Bochum that is centered around the Bermuda3Eck, a region with a lot of taverns, pubs, and clubs. Throughout the year, the city also holds festivals and live music performances.

The top areas in North Rhine-Westphalia for nightlife are only a few examples. Each city provides a variety of entertainment opportunities to suit various tastes and has its own distinct ambiance.

North Rhine-Westphalia is a diverse region in Germany that offers a wide variety of alcoholic beverages. Here are some soft and quality alcoholic drinks that are popular and suitable for consumption in North Rhine-Westphalia:

Kölsch: Kölsch is a top-fermented, pale beer that has its roots in Cologne (Köln). It has a taste that is a little bit fruity and is a light, crisp, and pleasant beer. In pubs and beer gardens all around North Rhine-Westphalia, Kölsch is a preferred beverage and is often served in tiny glasses called "Stangen."

Alt: In North Rhine-Westphalia, especially in the cities of Düsseldorf and the Ruhr area, alt is a different traditional beer type that is well-liked. Alt is a top-fermented beer that is dark, copper in color, and has a malty flavor and a little bitter aftertaste. It has a rich, full-bodied flavor and is often served in tiny, cylindrical glasses.

Riesling: North Rhine-Westphalia, particularly the areas around the Rhine and Mosel rivers, produces top-notch Riesling wines. Riesling is a white grape type that may be either dry or sweet and is renowned for its fragrant features. The Rieslings from this area are recognized for their bright fruit flavors, sharp acidity, and floral undertones.

Apfelwein is a traditional German cider produced from fermented apples, also called as Ebbelwoi in the region. Hessen, which borders North Rhine-Westphalia, is where it is most well-liked. The traditional apple wine taverns (Apfelweinlokale) that can be found in places like Frankfurt and Wiesbaden serve apfelwein, which has a tart, refreshing flavor.

A transparent, distilled alcohol known as korn is created from fermented grains like rye, wheat, or barley. Though it has a different taste character, it is related to vodka. In Germany's western areas, such as North Rhine-Westphalia, korn is widely enjoyed either straight or included into cocktails.

Kräuterlikör: For those looking for a tasty and fragrant beverage, herbal liqueur, also known as Kräuterlikör, is a popular option. Herbal liqueurs are often taken as digestifs or added to drinks by companies like Jägermeister and Underberg. These liqueurs often include an assortment of herbs, spices, and botanicals, giving them a flavor that is complex and herbaceous.

While not unique to North Rhine-Westphalia, weizenbier, or wheat beer, is nonetheless a preferred beverage here. Unfiltered weizenbier is a crisp beer prepared with a sizable amount of malted wheat. It has an unusually hazy look and often tastes delicious and spicy with hints of banana and clove.

Keep in mind to consume alcoholic drinks sensibly and in compliance with local laws governing the legal drinking age.

North Rhine-Westphalia is a state in Germany known for its rich cultural heritage, vibrant cities, and beautiful landscapes. Here are some interesting places to visit in North Rhine-Westphalia:

One of Germany's most recognizable sights is the magnificent Gothic Cologne Cathedral (Kölner Dom).

Schloss Benrath is a gorgeous Baroque house with lovely grounds around it that is situated near Düsseldorf.

Charlemagne's tomb, the Aachen Cathedral, is a UNESCO World Heritage Site with stunning architecture.

Former coal mine in Essen that is now home to museums and exhibits is known as the Zollverein Coal Mine Industrial Complex.

Drachenfels: A mountain close to Bonn with magnificent views of the Rhine Valley and a historic fortress.

Westfalenpark: A sizable park in Dortmund that is renowned for its lovely plants, play areas, and the Florian Tower with its expansive views.

The magnificent baroque house Schloss Nordkirchen, sometimes referred to as the "Versailles of Westphalia," has sizable gardens and water features.

Museum Ludwig: A modern and contemporary art museum in Cologne with a sizable collection.

Phantasialand is a well-known theme park in Brühl with exhilarating rides, entertaining performances, and themed zones.

Königswinter is a quaint Rhine River village that offers boat tours, hiking paths, and the renowned Drachenburg Castle.

In Dortmund, there is a well-preserved coal mine called Zeche Zollern that is now a museum reflecting the area's industrial past.

Burg Vischering is a charming moated castle near Lüdinghausen that offers excursions and a look into the Middle Ages.

The picturesque Römer-Lippe-Route winds across North Rhine-Westphalia, retracing the steps of the Romans.

A large collection of European artwork from many eras is housed at Düsseldorf's Museum Kunstpalast.

The Deutsches Eck is a landmark in Koblenz that overlooks the confluence of the Rhine and Moselle rivers and offers cable car rides and panoramic views.

These are just a handful of the numerous fascinating locations in North Rhine-Westphalia. There are several historical, cultural, and natural things to discover in the state.

list of generally affordable food options that are commonly found in North Rhine-Westphalia, Germany.
Here are five relatively affordable food items:

Currywurst is a well-known German fast food item that consists of a sliced sausage served with curry ketchup and often French fries. It is a typical and inexpensive kind of street cuisine.

Döner kebab: Döner kebab is a popular Germanized version of a Turkish meal. Usually served in a bread roll with salad, sauce, and sometimes fries, it consists of grilled meat (usually lamb or chicken). It often comes at reasonable price ranges.

German sausages produced from beef, veal, or pig are called bratwurst. It is often served with mustard and a side of bread or sauerkraut. Depending on the institution, bratwurst may be found at different pricing ranges.

Schnitzel: A schnitzel is a cutlet of breaded and fried meat, often prepared from veal or pig. It often comes with a side of potatoes or fries, along with a salad. Even while costs might vary, many eateries provide budget-friendly choices.

Brezeln, or pretzels in German, are a well-liked baked snack. They are often available in bakeries, stalls on the street, and even supermarkets. Pretzels are often cheap and make for a tasty snack.

Remember that prices might change, so it's a good idea to constantly check with neighborhood businesses for the most recent details on pricing.

CHAPTER 2.

German state of North Rhine-Westphalia is renowned for its industrialized cities and picturesque scenery. Although there are no coastal regions, there are a number of lakes and manmade beaches that provide sensations similar to those found on a beach. Here are five well-known ones:

Baldeneysee Beach in Essen is a sandy beach that provides a stunning setting with crystal-clear waters and lovely surroundings. It is situated on the banks of Lake Baldeney. Swimming, tanning, and water activities are all quite popular there.

Aasee Beach in Münster is a great place to get away from the city. Aasee is a sizable lake in Münster. The sandy beach is great for unwinding, picnicking, and swimming in the cool waves.

Beach at Halterner Stausee (Haltern am See): The Halterner Stausee is a reservoir close to the community of Haltern am See. Swimming, sailing, and windsurfing are among the many leisure activities at this area's well-kept beach.

Another beach on Lake Baldeney, Seaside Beach Baldeney (Essen) provides a tropical ambiance with its sand beach, palm trees, and water sports amenities. Beach volleyball matches, summer picnics, and other activities are often held there.

Though technically not in North Rhine-Westphalia, Wachtendonk is home to the Blaue Lagune (Blue Lagoon), which is just over the border from Krefeld. Originally a sand quarry, it has been turned into a gorgeous turquoise lake with sandy beaches, making it a well-liked spot for diving, swimming, and sunbathing.

North Rhine-Westphalia, located in western Germany, is home to several popular parks that offer a variety of recreational activities and natural beauty. Here are some of the well-known parks in North Rhine-Westphalia:

Dortmund's Westfalenpark is a sizable park renowned for its plentiful greenery, vibrant flower arrangements, and recreational amenities. Throughout the year, it holds a lot of festivals and events.

Grugapark in Essen is a sizable park with nicely planted gardens, a sizable playground, walking paths, and a lake. Additionally, it has a botanical garden and holds several horticultural and cultural events.

Volksgarten (Düsseldorf): Volksgarten is a charming park in Düsseldorf that is renowned for its serenity and immaculate gardens. It has a wonderful pond, strolling trails, and wide green areas.

Located in Cologne along the Rhine River, Rheinpark is a well-liked leisure area with breathtaking views of the river and the cityscape. There are many of green spaces there, as well as trails for walking and bicycling and picnic places.

Aasee Park in Münster: Aasee Park is a lovely park that is situated in Münster. Boating, fishing, cycling, and strolling are all permitted around the Aasee Lake. The park, which has a beach area as well, is a well-liked destination for entertainment and relaxation.

The Botanischer Garten in Bochum is a botanical garden that exhibits a vast range of plant species from all over the globe. It has pristine gardens, greenhouses, and instructive displays.

Schlosspark Benrath (Düsseldorf): The Schlosspark Benrath is a park that is located around the Benrath Palace. It has antique structures, lush gardens, classy walkways, a lovely pond, and more.

Stadtgarten (Cologne): The Stadtgarten is a charming urban park in the center of Cologne that is well-known for its luxuriant vegetation, vibrant flowerbeds, and outdoor entertainment. From the busy city core, it provides a tranquil retreat.

Grugapark Hagen (Hagen): Grugapark Hagen is a sizable park in Hagen with plenty of open space, strolling paths, and a sizable pond. Throughout the year, it holds events and exhibits and provides a variety of leisure activities.

North Rhine-Westphalia (NRW) is a state in Germany known for its vibrant economy and diverse industries. Here are five profitable businesses that are affordable to start up in NRW:

Starting an e-commerce site may be a successful business decision given the rising popularity of online purchasing. Create an online shop using tools like Shopify or WooCommerce and pinpoint a specialized market or distinctive product. To thrive in this cutthroat industry, put an emphasis on effective marketing methods, top-notch customer service, and swift order fulfillment.

Local Food Delivery Service: Launch a local food delivery company to take advantage of the growing need for convenient meal delivery services. Partner with neighborhood eateries and act as their delivery service. To succeed in this market, invest in a dependable delivery fleet, develop an intuitive website or ordering app, and give outstanding customer service.

Craft Brewery: The demand for craft beer has increased significantly in recent years, and NRW boasts a vibrant beer scene. Open a craft brewery and make distinctive, top-notch beer to satisfy local preferences. Aim to create a welcoming taproom atmosphere, work with nearby companies to host events, and forge strong connections with distributors and merchants.

Opening a shop that focuses on eco-friendly apparel and accessories might be a successful business concept given the growing customer desire for sustainable and ethical fashion. Purchase goods from regional designers and global companies recognized for their eco-friendly business methods. Participate in regional fashion events and exhibits, and promote your store as a destination for ethical shoppers.

Fitness Studio: As the significance of health and wellbeing increases, starting a fitness studio may be a successful business. Create a studio that provides specialized lessons in one or more unique fitness specialties, such as yoga, Pilates, or high-intensity interval training (HIIT). Create a warm and inspiring atmosphere for your customers by purchasing high-quality equipment, hiring qualified teachers, and doing so.

Researching the market, creating a strong business strategy, collecting money if necessary, acquiring the required licenses and permissions, and adhering to local laws are all crucial factors to take into account when beginning any kind of company in NRW. To secure long-term prosperity, also ensure that you stay abreast of market changes, advertise your company successfully, and provide first-rate customer service.

Detailed schedule to spend a good, decent, safe, functioning, Healthy and wealthy life in NORTH RHINE-WESTPHALIA.

Consideration of many elements of life, including as employment, leisure, health, money, and personal development, would need the creation of a thorough timetable for living a good, decent, safe, functional, healthy, and affluent life in North Rhine-Westphalia. To get you started, here is an example schedule:

Daily Schedule:

Wake up at six in the morning and sip some water.
Exercise for 30 minutes, such as yoga or running, around 6:15 in the morning.
Take a revitalizing shower around 6:45 AM and then get dressed.

41

Have a healthy meal at seven in the morning that includes fruits, whole grains, and proteins.

Start your commute to work or work from home routine at 7:30 AM.

Schedule of Work:

6. Get to work at 8:00 a.m., concentrating on your most significant assignments.

10:00 A.M.: Take a little break and stretch to prevent excessive sitting.

12:30 PM: Savor a balanced lunch, ideally one you cooked yourself or one you can get nearby.

1:30 PM: Get back to work, work with colleagues, and go to meetings.

3:30 PM: Enjoy a little break and a nutritious food to help you refresh.

5:00 PM: Finish up today's work and make plans for tomorrow.

Afternoon Routine:

12. 5:30 PM: Enjoy some downtime by reading, enjoying a hobby, or spending time with close friends and family.

6:30 PM: Make a healthful supper using items from your neighborhood.

7:30 PM: Enjoy supper with loved ones or friends, putting an emphasis on spending time together and talking.

8:30 PM: Relax with restorative practices like meditation or a hot bath.

9:00 PM: Schedule time for personal improvement activities, such picking up a new skill or reading knowledge-based material.

10 o'clock: Establish a nighttime routine to get 7-8 hours of unbroken sleep.

Dates for the weekend: 18. Saturdays: Set aside some time to take in North Rhine-Westphalia's scenic and cultural attractions. Take day excursions to surrounding cities or go to parks and museums.

Sundays should be devoted to self-care and personal renewal. Practice mindfulness, be creative, spend time with loved ones, and make plans for the next week.

20. Financial planning. To manage and examine your money, set aside time each month. Cost-benefit analysis, budgeting, goal-saving, and judicious investment are all important. If necessary, think about getting expert counsel.

Give regular medical exams, dental cleanings, and immunizations a priority.

Obtain at least 150 minutes of physical exercise each week by participating in activities like cycling, swimming, or fitness courses.

Maintain a nutritious diet by include whole grains, lean meats, fresh fruits and vegetables, and healthy fats.

Set aside time for stress-relieving hobbies and relaxation strategies like meditation or joyful pursuits.

Personal Development: 25. Take advantage of possibilities for continuing education or professional development to improve your abilities.

To broaden your network and meet like-minded people locally, join community clubs or organisations.

Attend seminars on subjects that interest you, read books about them, or listen to podcasts.

To give back to the community, take part in volunteer work or philanthropic endeavors.

North Rhine-Westphalia (NRW) is the largest state in Germany and is home to several prominent marketplaces. Here are some of the best marketplaces in North Rhine-Westphalia:

Kölner Weihnachtsmarkt, often known as the Cologne Christmas Market, is a well-known Christmas market that draws millions of tourists each year with its festive atmosphere, a wide variety of booths offering goods like as crafts, food, and beverages, and a stunning view of the Cologne Cathedral in the background.

Düsseldorf Christmas Market (Düsseldorfer Weihnachtsmarkt): In the heart of Düsseldorf, there is a wonderful Christmas market. It offers a broad selection of local and foreign cuisine, as well as artistically adorned booths, a sizable ice rink, and a Ferris wheel.

The Dortmund Christmas Market, also known as the Dortmund Weihnachtsmarkt, is one of the biggest in NRW. There are several booths, a big Christmas tree, entertainment events, and a huge variety of food and beverages available.

The Zollverein Coal Mine Industrial Complex, which is inscribed on the UNESCO World Heritage List, provides the setting for the Essen Christmas Market (Essener Weihnachtsmarkt). The industrial background gives it a particular feel as it displays handicrafts, local specialties, and one-of-a-kind items.

Aachen's Christmas market, or Aachener Weihnachtsmarkt, is renowned for its historic setting and close proximity to the magnificent Aachen Cathedral. It has a mix of conventional and contemporary vendors, delectable regional delicacies like Aachener Printen (gingerbread), and a nostalgic ambiance.

Medienhafen Flohmarkt, Düsseldorf - This flea market is located in Düsseldorf's hip Medienhafen neighborhood. It has a variety of vintage apparel, antiques, books, records, and other distinctive goods, making it a gold mine for collectors and deal seekers.

A well-known retail complex in Cologne is called KölnArcaden. It is a great one-stop location for shoppers since it has a variety of shops, boutiques, and restaurants.

Every Wednesday and Saturday, one of the oldest weekly markets in Germany, Münster Wochenmarkt, is open to the public. It provides a huge selection of local delicacies, fresh fruit, flowers, and crafts.

The greatest markets in North Rhine-Westphalia may be found in areas like these. There are several more markets worth visiting, each with its own distinctive charm and attractions. The area is famed for its bustling marketplaces.

North Rhine-Westphalia, located in western Germany, is home to several beautiful churches and religious sites. Here are some of the notable churches in the region:

The Gothic masterpiece known as the Cologne Cathedral (Kölner Dom) is one of Germany's most well-known structures, a UNESCO World Heritage site, and a well-known landmark in the city of Cologne.

German monarchs were crowned at the Aachen Cathedral, also known as the Aachener Dom, which is a UNESCO World Heritage Site. It holds the Palatine Chapel and is renowned for its Carolingian architecture.

The 14th-century Romanesque-style church known as St. Lambertus Basilica is located in Düsseldorf and is distinguished by its twisting tower.

The interior and mosaics of the Basilica of St. Gereon in Cologne are among its most beautiful features. It is one of Cologne's oldest churches.

St. Maria am Kapitol, a Romanesque church in Cologne, is well-known for its elaborate golden shrine and exquisite murals. It is situated close to the Rhine River.

St. Paulus Dom in Münster is the city's principal cathedral and a magnificent example of Gothic design. It also has imposing stained glass windows.

One of the oldest ecclesiastical structures in Germany is the Essen Cathedral (Essener Münster), which is located in the city of Essen. Romanesque and Gothic elements are combined in it.

St. Aposteln in Cologne is a Romanesque church with a stunning interior decoration that is well-known for its high altar and medieval artwork.

St. Maria zur Wiese in Soest is a Late Gothic hall church renowned for its elaborate wood carvings and breathtaking stained glass windows.

St. Viktor Dom) in Xanten, Germany: With its spectacular vaulted ceilings and beautiful interior, the cathedral in the town of Xanten is a noteworthy example of Lower Rhine Gothic architecture.

These are just a handful of North Rhine-Westphalia's many noteworthy churches. The area has a long history of religion, provides a variety of architectural styles, and is significant culturally.

CHAPTER 3.

Several banks are active and provide consumers financial services in North Rhine-Westphalia, Germany. While it is difficult to pinpoint the "best" banks with certainty, I can provide you a list of well-liked and well-known banks in the area. In order to make an educated choice, it is advised to do further research on each bank since popularity and performance might differ. Listed below are some of North Rhine-Westphalia's well-known banks:

Deutsche Bank: With multiple locations throughout North Rhine-Westphalia, Deutsche Bank is one of the biggest banks in Germany. Personal banking, business banking, wealth management, and investment banking are just a few of the many financial services it provides.

Commerzbank: Another prominent bank operating in Germany, Commerzbank has a considerable presence in North Rhine-Westphalia. Current accounts, loans, mortgages, investment alternatives, and corporate banking solutions are just a few of the many financial goods and services it offers.

The German savings bank network Sparkasse operates all throughout the country. Various Sparkasse branches in North Rhine-Westphalia serve various cities and towns. In addition to accounts, loans, mortgages, investments, and insurance, Sparkasse also provides personal and commercial banking services.

In North Rhine-Westphalia, there are a large number of Volksbanken and Raiffeisenbanken that provide cooperative banking services. These regionally oriented cooperative banks provide a variety of financial services, including as personal and business banking, loans, savings accounts, and investments.

DZ Bank: In Germany, DZ Bank serves as the nation's main cooperative banking hub. Along with cooperative banks in North Rhine-Westphalia, it offers financial services to them. The activities of DZ Bank indirectly help the cooperative banking industry in the area even if the bank itself does not directly service any particular consumers.

North Rhine-Westphalia residents may access ING-DiBa's services nationwide via the direct bank's website, which it principally manages. It offers a range of financial products, including loans, investment choices, current accounts, savings accounts, and loans.

North Rhine-Westphalia is home to many Postbank locations, which are a part of the Deutsche Bank group of companies. It provides many financial services, such as current and savings accounts, loans, mortgages, and investment choices.

The well-known banks that are active in North Rhine-Westphalia are only a few examples. It's wise to think about your unique banking requirements, compare the services, costs, and features provided by other banks, and visit their websites or locations for additional in-depth information.

A Day in North Rhine-Westphalia: Exploring the Vibrant Heart of Germany.

Germany's westernmost state, North Rhine-Westphalia, is vibrant and full of cultural diversity. This area is a nexus of economic activity, historical importance, and natural beauty, with busy cities and peaceful countryside. Join us as we explore a day packed with fascinating aspects of the routine activities of the nation in North Rhine-Westphalia.

Morning: Exploring the City's Cultural Heritage
North Rhine-Westphalia's cities spring to life with a hum of activity as the sun rises over the region. Start your day in the capital city of Düsseldorf, which is renowned for its mix of modern architecture and quaint charm. Take a walk along the Rhine promenade while

taking in the breathtaking river views and the recognizable Rheinturm. Explore the colorful Altstadt (Old Town), which has quaint streets, age-old breweries, and bustling cafés.

Go to Cologne next, which is known for its magnificent Cologne Cathedral. Climb to the summit for a stunning panoramic view of the city while admiring the beautiful Gothic architecture. Experience history firsthand at the Wallraf-Richartz Museum, which has a sizable collection of European art, or at the Roman-Germanic Museum, which houses ancient antiquities.

Nature and recreation in the afternoon
Go to North Rhine-Westphalia's serene landscapes to get away from the city's bustle. Travel to the Teutoburg Forest, a sizable forested region that offers scenic hiking routes, quaint towns, and

historical sites. Discover the Hermannsdenkmal, a massive monument honoring the Battle of the Teutoburg Forest, or relax next to the peaceful stream at the scenic Externsteine rock formations.

Alternately, go to the magnificent Eifel National Park, which is home to thick woods, picturesque lakes, and gushing waterfalls. Enjoy the peace and quiet of nature by going on a walk along the scenic paths, seeing animals, or taking a boat ride around the Rursee lake.

Evening: Cultural Wonders and Culinary Adventures
Enjoy the cultural splendors and culinary marvels of North Rhine-Westphalia as darkness falls. Come back to Düsseldorf, known for its gastronomic and fashion scenes. visit the vibrant MedienHafen neighborhood, noted for its eye-catching

contemporary architecture and hip bars, or visit the "Kö," an opulent retail strip packed with upscale stores.

Experience a gastronomic experience by indulging in regional delicacies like Currywurst or Rheinischer Sauerbraten at one of the quaint taverns or cutting-edge Michelin-starred restaurants. Drink an Altbier, a typical dark beer made only in Düsseldorf, to go with your dinner, which is locally produced.

Entertainment and nightlife at night
A variety of entertainment alternatives are available in North Rhine-Westphalia to round off your day. Enjoy a spectacular performance at the famous Cologne Opera House or go to one of the other theaters and music venues in Cologne that provide a wide variety of performances. Alternately, take in the

vibrant nightlife Düsseldorf has to offer, complete with hip pubs, clubs, and live music venues.

A day in North Rhine-Westphalia is an enjoyable tour through natural beauty, cultural history, and thriving urban life. This part of Germany has much to offer any tourist, from the museums and historical sites to the peaceful woodlands and bustling cities. Learn more about the heart and spirit of North Rhine-Westphalia, a region where tradition and modernity coexist in a riveting way that creates a lasting impact.

In North Rhine-Westphalia, Germany, several cultural festivals take place throughout the year. Here are some of the notable cultural festival seasons in North Rhine-Westphalia:

Karneval (Carnival): This traditional event, which is celebrated in February or March, features vibrant parades, costumes, music, and street parties. Karneval festivities are particularly lively in Cologne, Düsseldorf, and Aachen.

During the summer, North Rhine-Westphalia hosts the well-known shooting event known as Schützenfest in a number of its towns and cities. It includes sporting events, parades, live music, and traditional attire.

Kirmes: Throughout North Rhine-Westphalia, Kirmes is a

summertime ritual that takes place in several cities and villages. It offers games, amusement rides, food stands, and entertainment for people of all ages.

Christopher Street Day (CSD) is an LGBTQ+ pride celebration held in a number of North Rhine-Westphalian communities each summer. It entails events including parades, parties, cultural gatherings, and advocacy campaigns for the visibility and rights of LGBTQ+ people.

The Ruhrtriennale is a well-known arts festival that takes place every year in North Rhine-Westphalia's Ruhr district. In distinctive industrial settings, it presents a broad spectrum of modern performing arts, such as theater, dance, music, and visual arts.

Weihnachtsmarkt: In North Rhine-Westphalia, there are a variety of attractive Christmas markets that take place throughout the Advent season leading up to Christmas. There is a fantastic mood at these markets because to the lively vendors offering crafts, presents, food, and beverages.

The currency used in North Rhine-Westphalia, as well as the rest of Germany, is the Euro (€). The Euro is the official currency of Germany and is used in all states, including North Rhine-Westphalia.

Germany has a state called North Rhine-Westphalia. The euro (€) is the official currency of Germany, a member of the European Union (EU). North Rhine-Westphalia's monetary policies would be consistent with those of Germany and the ECB. Here are some essential details about the euro and Germany's monetary policies:

Euro (€) is the used currency.

European Central Bank (ECB) is the monetary authority.

Germany is a part of the Eurozone, which is where the ECB is in charge of establishing and carrying out monetary policy. Maintaining price stability and assisting the broader economic policy of the EU are the ECB's key goals.

Exchange Rate: The euro region has a fixed exchange rate system that applies to Germany as a member. The market factors that affect the euro's exchange rate versus other currencies are subject to change.

Currency conversion: Euro banknotes and coins are accepted for everyday transactions in North Rhine-Westphalia, as well as the rest of Germany. Banks, exchange bureaus, and certain financial institutions all provide the ability to exchange foreign currencies.

Membership in the Eurozone: Germany has been a part of the Eurozone since its formation. The Eurozone is made up of 19 EU members who have made the euro their national currency.

Please be advised that monetary and economic policies are subject to change throughout time. I advise consulting official government sources or getting in touch with the appropriate financial authorities for the most current and detailed information on currency policy in North Rhine-Westphalia or any other area.

Dressing outfits suitable in North Rhine-Westphalia.

It's crucial to consider the region's climate, cultural standards, and various fashion trends while thinking about how to dress for North Rhine-Westphalia. In western Germany's North Rhine-Westphalia region, the climate is moderate, with pleasant to chilly winters and warm summers. Here are a few costume suggestions for North Rhine-Westphalia that are appropriate for various events and seasons:

Women's Spring Casual Outfits: Team a floral-printed dress with a sheer cardigan, a pair of ankle boots, and a crossbody purse. On chilly days, throw on a denim jacket.
Men should put on a light-colored blazer, chinos, and a button-down shirt in a soft tone.

Women should choose a flowy sundress or jumpsuit and accessorize with sandals, a wide-brimmed hat, and sunglasses for a chic summer look. For a touch of summer, carry a straw tote bag.

Men should wear shorts, a linen or cotton shirt, boat shoes, and a straw fedora. Add sunglasses and a tote bag made of canvas.

Women's Autumn Fashion Classic: Wear a trench coat with jeans, ankle boots, and a thick sweater. Put on some jewelry and carry a leather tote bag.

To wear with a blazer, men should wear a button-down shirt, dark pants, and leather boots. For a refined appearance, add a scarf and a messenger bag.

Women should dress warmly during the winter by layering a wool coat over a turtleneck sweater, trousers, and high boots. A crossbody bag, gloves, and a beanie are essentials.

For men, put on a wool pea coat, a sweater, some pants, and some leather boots. Add gloves, a backpack, and a beanie to complete the outfit.

Remember that you may alter these clothing choices to suit your own tastes and certain circumstances. Before picking an outfit, be sure to check the weather forecast to verify that it will be appropriate for the day and comfortable.

CHAPTER 4.

NRW Zoos: Wildlife Wonderland.

Greetings and welcome to North Rhine-Westphalia's Zoos, a wildlife wonderland.

In addition to its economic success, the German state of North Rhine-Westphalia is renowned for its abundant natural beauty and dedication to wildlife preservation. The region is home to numerous top-notch zoological parks that provide tourists an unrivaled chance to get up close and personal with various species of animals. The zoos in North Rhine-Westphalia provide an engaging and educational experience for visitors of all ages, with everything from exotic animals from far-off regions to local species indigenous to Germany.

1. Cologne Zoo (Kölner Zoo): One of Germany's oldest and most recognized zoological parks, the Cologne Zoo is located in the center of Cologne. More than 10,000 animals from around 700 distinct species are housed at the zoo, which covers an area of more than 20 hectares. The Elephant Park, where Asian elephants may be seen ambling around a large, realistic environment, is one of its attractions. Additionally, the Cologne Zoo is a pioneer in conservation initiatives and takes part in various breeding projects to protect endangered species.

2. Duisburg Zoo (Zoo Duisburg): The Duisburg Zoo is one of the biggest and most species-diverse zoos in North Rhine-Westphalia. The zoo's habitats are designed to closely resemble the natural habitats of its residents. It is situated along the picturesque Rhine River. It is

renowned for its magnificent dolphin and sea lion performances, where guests can see the extraordinary intellect and agility of these aquatic species.

3. Wuppertal Zoo (Zoo Wuppertal): Nestled in the lovely Wuppertal valley, this endearing zoo provides visitors a unique experience since it is constructed on a hillside. In addition to increasing the excitement and offering breathtaking vistas, the famous suspended monorail known as the Schwebebahn runs right through the zoo. Red pandas, large cats, and other exotic bird species are among the creatures kept in the Wuppertal Zoo, which is a relatively modest facility.

4. Aachen Zoo (Aachener Tierpark): Aachen Zoo is a popular attraction for animal lovers and is situated not far from the borders of Belgium and the Netherlands. The zoo places a priority on

providing animals with natural habitats, resulting in a stimulating environment for both animals and visitors. It is an excellent location for family vacations and educational experiences since it has a mix of exotic and domestic animals.

5. Krefeld Zoo (Zoo Krefeld): The Krefeld Zoo is a treasure in North Rhine-Westphalia, with its roomy and well constructed habitats. The zoo, which is renowned for its effective breeding initiatives, has played a crucial role in preserving endangered species like the Sumatran tiger and orangutans. Also open to visitors is the tropical house, which is home to a wide variety of reptiles, amphibians, and tropical plants.

6. Bochum Tierpark (Tierpark Bochum): The care of animals and public education are top priorities at this zoological garden in Bochum. The Bochum Tierpark

focuses on native German species, allowing visitors to understand and enjoy the variety of local fauna. It's a great location for anyone who like the outdoors and are curious in the local wildlife.

These zoos in North Rhine-Westphalia not only provide tourists experiences they won't forget, but they also have a big impact on animal conservation and education. They aid in the preservation of endangered species by their work in breeding programs, research, and public education, and they serve as an inspiration to younger generations to value and safeguard the natural environment. Therefore, the zoos in North Rhine-Westphalia have something unique to offer to everyone, whether you are a wildlife lover, a family seeking a pleasant adventure, or someone looking to learn more about animals and their environments.

NRW School Education Guide

Welcome to the North Rhine-Westphalia Schools website in Germany.

Germany's North Rhine-Westphalia (NRW) is a diversified and dynamic area known for its extensive history, thriving culture, and top-notch educational system. In this guide, we'll examine NRW's educational system, highlighting its schools and the distinctive qualities that set them apart.

Education System in NRW: The NRW education system is well-structured and complete, and it's intended to provide pupils access to high-quality learning opportunities. Primary education, secondary education, and postsecondary education make up its three tiers. Germany's numerous states, including NRW, are responsible for education, hence there are some regional differences in the curriculum and administrative elements.

Primary Education: The first stage of education, or "Grundschule," is required for all pupils in the federal state of NRW. From the age of six to ten, students often attend Grundschule. Teaching fundamental abilities including reading, writing, arithmetic, and fostering social skills are the main objectives of this era.

Secondary Education: After graduating from Grundschule, students continue their education at this level. NRW provides a variety of secondary school programs:

Hauptschule: Students who attend this kind of school are prepared for entry-level employment or vocational training by focusing on practical skills.

Realschule: Realschule is a learning environment that falls in between Hauptschule and Gymnasium, emphasizing both theoretical and practical knowledge.

Gymnasium: A Gymnasium is a high school that focuses on academics and prepares pupils for a university admission exam called the Abitur.

In order to accommodate students of all capacities under one roof, the Gesamtschule is a comprehensive school that integrates all three secondary education options.

Exams for the Abitur and university education are available to students who have completed their secondary school, notably from Gymnasium. If they pass these examinations, they may enroll in colleges and universities for further study.

School Days and Extracurricular Activities: In NRW, the average school day schedule consists of a combination of classroom teaching, recess, and extracurricular activities. In NRW, schools often encourage students to join organizations, sports teams, and cultural activities to promote personal growth and a feeling of community.

School Resources and Infrastructure: NRW schools benefit from a cutting-edge infrastructure and easy access to a wealth of learning materials. They place a high priority on establishing learning environments that are comfortable and furnished with modern technology and libraries.

Language and multiculturalism: NRW is renowned for its cultural richness, and the educational system reflects this effectively. Language learning opportunities for students include learning English, French, Spanish, and other languages. Schools also encourage cross-cultural understanding and celebrate diversity.

Inclusive Education: In order to meet the requirements of students with a range of learning capacities, NRW puts a strong focus on inclusive education. Every student has equitable access to high-quality education because to the special education services and support that are available.

The intellectual, social, and personal development of children is fostered in North Rhine-Westphalia schools, which provide a complete and inclusive education. The school system in NRW is dedicated to quality and continues to pave the way for the area's bright and optimistic future with cutting-edge facilities and a diversified cultural environment.

Airport in North Rhine-Westphalia, Germany

Numerous airports in North Rhine-Westphalia, a thriving and populated area of Germany, are essential for linking the state with the rest of the globe. These airports act as busy transportation hubs for both domestic and international travel, tourism, and economic development. Let's examine a few of North Rhine-Westphalia's well-known airports:

The biggest and busiest airport in North Rhine-Westphalia is Düsseldorf Airport (DUS), which is situated in the state capital of Düsseldorf. With multiple airlines providing flights to different locations across the world, it acts as a significant gateway to the area. Modern terminals, stores, dining areas, and lounges are just a few of the cutting-edge amenities that DUS has to offer, making for a comfortable trip for travellers.

2. Cologne-Bonn Airport (CGN): This international airport is another important air travel hub in North Rhine-Westphalia and is located close to the towns of Cologne and Bonn. A significant amount of both passenger and freight traffic is handled by CGN, which is also famous for its effective management and superior connection. The airport is a crucial connection for both business and leisure visitors because to its advantageous location.

3. Dortmund Airport (DTM): Located in North Rhine-Westphalia's eastern area, Dortmund Airport is a regional airport serving both domestic and international travel. DTM is crucial in providing Ruhr area inhabitants with easy air travel

alternatives, although not being as big as Düsseldorf or Cologne Bonn.

4. Münster Osnabrück International Airport (FMO): Located in the state's northern portion and serving the Münsterland and Osnabrück regions, FMO is a crucial regional airport. Despite handling a lesser volume of flights than the larger airports, it offers vital air connections for nearby visitors and companies.

5. Weeze Airport (NRN): Previously known as Niederrhein Airport, Weeze Airport is a low-cost carrier hub in North Rhine-Westphalia and is situated close to the Dutch border. It draws tourists looking for low-cost travel choices by providing flights to many European locations.

In addition to serving passenger flights, these airports have a large economic impact on the state through handling cargo, which generates jobs and promotes economic development. Traveling to and from these airports is simple and easy because to their contemporary amenities, adequate parking, and effective ground transportation connections.

North Rhine-Westphalia's airports are constantly developing to meet the demands of passengers and the aviation industry. They continue to be essential parts of the state's infrastructure, contributing significantly to the promotion of foreign relations, tourism, and economic growth thanks to their advantageous positions and first-rate connection.

Exploring the Enchanting Forests of North Rhine-Westphalia

Germany's North Rhine-Westphalia region, which is in the country's west, is home to some of the nation's most beautiful and varied natural settings. These forests, which cover large regions, are very diverse and full of historical, cultural, and recreational activities. The woods of North Rhine-Westphalia have something special to offer everyone, whether they are ardent nature lovers, adventure-seeking hikers, or animal enthusiasts. Come along on a trip with us as we explore these breathtaking natural beauties and unearth their hidden secrets.

The Teutoburg woodland, sometimes referred to as "Teutoburger Wald," is a beautiful and historic woodland situated in the eastern region of North Rhine-Westphalia. This woods combines cultural value with unmatched natural beauty. It is well-known for its connection to the historic Battle of the Teutoburg Forest in 9 AD. Visitors may explore a variety of hiking paths that take them to gorgeous overlooks, magnificent rock formations, and the well-known Hermannsdenkmal, a memorial honoring the Germanic leader Arminius.

The Eifel National Park is a protected region brimming with wildlife that is tucked away in North Rhine-Westphalia's southwest corner. Numerous species of animals may be found in this old woodland, including red deer, wildcats, and the rare black stork. For lovers of nature, the Eifel provides a peaceful retreat with its lush forests, quiet lakes, and flowing rivers. The park's educational facilities provide information on its ecological significance and conservation activities, and its many paths appeal to hikers of all skill levels.

The Rothaargebirge: The Rothaargebirge is a beautiful mountain range covered in dense woods that extends throughout the southern portion of the area. The Kahler Asten, one of the notable peaks in this area that provides expansive views of the surroundings, is one of the prominent summits. You could come upon historic castles, adorable towns, and secret tunnels as you meander through the lush vegetation, adding to the region's charm. Mountain biking, rock climbing, and winter sports are all popular outdoor pursuits in the Rothaargebirge.

The Arnsberg Forest: The Arnsberg Forest, which is close to Arnsberg, offers a lovely mixture of beech, oak, and pine forests. A favorite location for outdoor lovers, this wooded region is crisscrossed by well designated hiking and bicycle routes. A neighboring reservoir that offers boating, fishing, and birding possibilities is the Möhnesee, which nature enthusiasts may also visit. The woodland comes alive with colorful blossoms in the spring, creating a wonderful setting for a leisurely walk.

Each visitor may have a variety of experiences in North Rhine-Westphalia's woods, which are a treasure trove of natural beauty. These forests provide a retreat for anyone seeking peace and adventure, with their many historical landmarks, breathtaking views, abundant animals, and peaceful lakes. North Rhine-Westphalia's woods guarantee an amazing trip into the center of nature's marvels, whether you're learning about the history of the Teutoburg Forest or trekking through the thick Rothaargebirge. Pack your hiking boots and bag, then set off on a thrilling adventure through North Rhine-Westphalia's enchanted woodlands.

Annual Conference in North Rhine-Westphalia

The annual conference in North Rhine-Westphalia, which brings together professionals, experts, researchers, and fans from numerous businesses and areas, is a much-anticipated occasion. This conference offers a forum for sharing information, connecting with others, and working together to promote innovation and progress both within the local community and beyond.

Objective:

The Annual Conference's main goal is to provide attendees a place to exchange ideas, research results, best practices, and cutting-edge developments. The conference intends to promote debate and discussion on important topics, difficulties, and chances encountered by many industries.

Theme:

Every year, the conference chooses a particular topic to represent the most recent developments and needs in the relevant industry. The event's keynote speakers, workshop subjects, and presentation topics are all influenced by the theme that has been selected as a guiding concept.

Important Elements

Eminent figures from a range of fields provide motivational keynote addresses, providing insightful views on the subject and its significance for the development of the area.

Panels and Workshops: Interesting panel discussions and workshops are held, offering chances for in-depth investigation of certain topics. These seminars are led by professionals and experts, who promote problem-solving and participatory learning.

Research Presentations: Academics and researchers share their most recent discoveries and research, fostering interdisciplinary cooperation and enhancing the intellectual experience of participants.

Exhibitions and Demonstrations: An exhibition section features cutting-edge goods, services, and technology to provide visitors a hands-on learning opportunity and promote business prospects.

Sessions for networking: The conference offers plenty of chances for networking, allowing attendees to meet other professionals who share their interests, possible partners, and business leaders.

Awards & Recognitions: The event may include award ceremonies to recognize exceptional contributions and accomplishments in many fields, fostering excellence and innovation.

Social and Cultural Events: Social get-togethers and cultural events are planned to provide a welcoming and pleasurable environment that fosters friendship among participants.

Effects and Results:

The North Rhine-Westphalia Annual Conference has an enduring effect on the area and its stakeholders. Key results include the following:

Knowledge Exchange and Dissemination: Participants pick up fresh thoughts, information, and viewpoints that help them advance personally and professionally.

Networking and Partnerships: Those who attend make important contacts with prospective customers, partners, investors, and collaborators, strengthening business partnerships.

Keynote addresses and success stories motivate the audience, inspiring them to embark on new endeavors and creative strategies.

Community Building: By encouraging a climate of collaboration and mutual assistance, the conference develops the professional community in North Rhine-Westphalia.

Impact on the local economy: By displaying cutting-edge goods and services, the conference encourages investment and grows the regional economy.

The Annual Conference in North Rhine-Westphalia acts as a showcase occasion that promotes development, innovation, and cooperation amongst industries. The conference, which addresses both global possibilities and problems, plays a crucial role in determining the future of the area thanks to its compelling program and broad group of attendees. Even as the event changes, it is still a crucial forum for networking, exchanging information, and improving society as a whole.

Seas, ocean and river in North Rhine-Westphalia

West German state of North Rhine-Westphalia is renowned for its industrial hubs, cultural landmarks, and picturesque landscapes. Although North Rhine-Westphalia is not immediately on the shore, it does feature sizable river systems that are essential to the history, economics, and scenic beauty of the area. Let's find out more about the rivers, lakes, and seas in and around North Rhine-Westphalia:

Rivers:

One of the most significant rivers in Europe, the Rhine runs through North Rhine-Westphalia. It serves as the main waterway for the area and is important for travel, commerce, and tourism. Beautiful scenery, quaint communities, and important historical sites may be found along the river's banks.

Ruhr River: Running through the Ruhr region of North Rhine-Westphalia, the Ruhr River is a significant tributary of the Rhine. In the past, the industrialisation of the area was greatly influenced by the Ruhr. It now provides leisure activities and is a significant component of the local cultural history.

Seas and Oceans: Because North Rhine-Westphalia is an inland state, it lacks direct access to the seas or the oceans. The North Sea, the closest coastal region, is situated far from where it is.

Nevertheless, despite lacking coasts, North Rhine-Westphalia is home to a number of inland water features, including lakes and reservoirs, which provide possibilities for recreation, outdoor activities, and visual splendor. Lakes in the area that are well-known include:

Baldeneysee: This lake, which is close to Essen and was formed by damming the Ruhr River, is well-known for sailing, windsurfing, and other water sports.

Aasee is a beautiful lake located near Münster that offers recreational activities including boating and walking trails along its banks.

Phoenix See: A man-made lake created on the site of a former steel plant, the Phoenix See is located in Dortmund. It has gained popularity as a place for leisure and entertainment.

Sorpesee: Situated in the Sauerland area, Sorpesee is a reservoir with hiking, sailing, and swimming options along its banks.

Biggesee: Biggesee, a reservoir in the Sauerland region, offers a peaceful environment for boating and recreation.

The river systems, lakes, and reservoirs of North Rhine-Westphalia add to the allure of the area and its recreational opportunities, drawing in both inhabitants and tourists.

Caution: Late Nights in North Rhine-Westphalia

In order to protect your safety and wellbeing when you engage in nocturnal activities in North Rhine-Westphalia, it is crucial to be aware of a few safety considerations. Even though North Rhine-Westphalia is often a safe location, it's always best to be prepared and use care, especially late at night. Here are some thorough warnings to think about:

Plan your route: It's a good idea to have an itinerary in place before going out for late-night activities. Decide the regions you want to visit, then look into their safety records. When traveling in a new place, stay in well-known and frequented regions.

Stay in well-lit locations: When out at night, prefer well-lit areas with high pedestrian traffic. Avoid dimly lit or empty places since they can be more prone to criminal behavior. Learn the locations of the businesses, stations for the public transit, and well-lit streets.

Using public transit sensibly may help you get about North Rhine-Westphalia at night. Examples of such modes of transportation include buses, trams, and trains. When using these services, however, use caution. Avoid lonely or deserted stations, and if at all feasible, travel with others or a reliable friend. To avoid theft, remain watchful and aware of your possessions.

Be careful with personal items: Keep a tight check on your personal items, such as handbags, wallets, cell phones, and cameras, when visiting North Rhine-Westphalia at night. Keep pricey objects safe and out of sight while not in use. Avoid leaving your valuables unsecured and be wary of pickpockets in busy places.

Keep an eye on your surroundings: While engaging in late-night activities, situational awareness is essential. Pay attention to the individuals around you and any strange activity as you remain vigilant and aware of your surroundings. If you feel threatened, trust your instincts and stay away from conflict. Ask for help from local businesses or call the police if you feel uncomfortable.

Drink sensibly: It's important to drink sensibly if you want to consume alcohol throughout your late-night activities. Alcohol abuse might affect your judgment, making you more susceptible to mishaps or illegal activity. If you can't drive safely because of your health, take it slow, recognize your limitations, and think about other transportation choices.

Prepare for crises by ensuring that your phone is loaded with the necessary emergency contact information before leaving the house. Learn about the local emergency services, and have a backup plan ready in case anything unexpected happens. Give a family member or acquaintance you can trust a copy of your itinerary and keep them updated on your location and estimated time of return.

Please keep in mind that following suggestions are meant to increase safety during late-night events in North Rhine-Westphalia. It is usually a good idea to keep up with the latest developments about safety in the particular places you want to visit. Additionally, keeping up with regional news sources or asking for guidance from locals may provide you important insights into any specific worries or safety measures that apply to the area.

Prioritize your safety and wellbeing while having fun on your late-night excursions in North Rhine-Westphalia.

CONCLUSION.

In summary, North Rhine-Westphalia is a treasure mine of amazing experiences and magical locations that will enthrall any tourist. This German state provides a variety of attractions that are sure to suit every taste and inclination, from the dynamic cityscapes of Cologne and Düsseldorf to the scenic landscapes of the Rhine River and the Eifel area.

North Rhine-Westphalia has something to offer everyone, whether you're interested in history and want to explore the historic castles and quaint medieval villages, in art and want to take in the dynamic cultural scene, or you're an outdoor adventurer looking for exhilarating outdoor sports. A distinctive fusion of traditional charm and current excitement is produced by the state's rich historical history and modern, inventive energy.

Traveling around North Rhine-Westphalia is smooth and delightful thanks to the warm welcome of the inhabitants as well as the region's first-rate infrastructure and effective transportation system. The state's culinary landscape also entices foodies with a wide variety of traditional and foreign cuisines, making every meal a special gourmet adventure.

A trip to North Rhine-Westphalia would not be complete without taking in the state's renowned carnival celebrations, which bring the state to life with vibrant parades, upbeat music, and jubilant festivities. The vibrant attitude and happy character of the locals are on display during these events.

North Rhine-Westphalia will definitely make a lasting impression on your heart as you travel through the beautiful landscapes, discover the historical sites, indulge in the regional food, and immerse yourself in the vibrant culture. It is a place that welcomes you to embrace its rich history, take in its natural beauty, and learn about its dynamic spirit.

Pack your luggage, set off on a memorable adventure, and let North Rhine-Westphalia to enchant you with all of its delights. This magical area promises to provide a really immersive and satisfying experience that will leave you with treasured memories for a lifetime, whether you're a first-time visitor or an experienced tourist.

Printed in Great Britain
by Amazon

25683802R00066